Whispers of Self

Love, Loss, Renewal

Adelina C

ISBN 979-8-89673-741-4

Table of Contents

Introduction

Welcome to *Whispers of Self*, a sanctuary for those seeking solace, healing, and a deeper connection with themselves. This book is born from the belief that even amidst heartbreak and struggle, we can find moments of profound beauty and transformation. Through the tender art of poetry, reflective essays, and guided practices, this journey invites you to embrace the fullness of your emotions and rediscover the light within.

Life's challenges often leave us feeling fragmented and uncertain. Yet, it is within these cracks that the light of understanding and acceptance shines through. Each page of this manuscript is an offering—a gentle hand to hold as you navigate your unique path toward healing and self-awareness.

Here, you will find the wisdom of mindfulness, the courage to let go, and the grace to honor your journey. Whether through the simplicity of a poem or the depth of a reflective exercise, each element is crafted to nurture your spirit and inspire growth.

This is not just a book; it is an invitation. An invitation to pause, reflect, and discover the boundless strength and compassion that resides within you. May this be a companion as you embrace the whispers of your soul and awaken to the beauty of your true self.

Heartbreak's Echo

When our hearts are broken,
Mindfulness helps us see,
In each piece of our pain,
A chance to just be.

Flaws aren't just mistakes,
They're parts of who we are.
In accepting these rough edges,
We find our own star.

Embracing Heartbreak

Heartbreak is one of the most profound and challenging experiences we can endure. The emotional depth of heartache can feel suffocating, as if a heavy weight is pressing down on our chest. It's more than just sadness; it's a complex web of feelings that can include anger, confusion, and even guilt.

Experiencing heartache is a deeply personal journey. It often feels like navigating through a storm where the winds are relentless and the rain never seems to stop. This profound pain can make everyday tasks seem insurmountable, leaving us feeling isolated and overwhelmed. The struggle is real and ongoing as we attempt to piece ourselves back together.

Yet, within this pain lies an opportunity for profound growth and self-discovery. Acknowledging and sitting with our heartache allows us to understand ourselves on a deeper level. It's through this acceptance of our suffering that we find the strength to heal.

Personal Reflection:

I vividly remember the suffocating feeling of heartache after a significant loss. It felt like an emotional void that consumed every part of me. Each day was a struggle, and even simple tasks felt like monumental challenges. Through the process of acknowledging my pain, seeking support, and gradually finding moments of solace, I began to understand the resilience that emerged from such profound suffering. This experience, while difficult, taught me about my own capacity for endurance and growth.

1. What is your usual response to heartbreak? How can you approach it differently?
2. Reflect on a past heartbreak. What did you learn from that experience, and how did it shape you?
3. How can you support yourself emotionally during times of pain?

Mindful Journeys

- **Emotional Check-Ins:** Schedule regular times to check in with yourself about your feelings. Use a journal or a voice memo to express your emotions.
- **Healing Activities:** Engage in activities that bring you comfort and joy, such as reading, listening to music, or spending time in nature.
- **Support Network:** Reach out to friends or support groups regularly. Share your feelings and listen to others' experiences for mutual support.

The Quiet Space

In the quiet moments,
After the tears have dried,
Mindfulness shows us
Where our true selves hide.

We may not be perfect,
But that's okay.
In accepting our journey,
We find love every day.

The Path of Mindfulness

Mindfulness, while offering clarity and calm, does not erase the pain we experience. Instead, it helps us navigate it with greater awareness and acceptance. The journey of mindfulness is not always easy—it involves facing our inner turmoil and embracing it without judgment.

The practice of mindfulness requires us to be present with our emotions, even when they are overwhelming. It invites us to sit with our discomfort and observe it with curiosity rather than aversion. This process can be difficult as it often brings us face-to-face with feelings we might prefer to ignore or escape.

Through consistent mindfulness practice, we learn to approach our pain with compassion. We start to see that our suffering is a natural part of being human and that it does not define us. This shift in perspective allows us to find peace amidst the chaos and build a foundation for healing.

Personal Anecdote:

During a particularly stressful period, I found that mindfulness helped me acknowledge and embrace my emotional pain rather than avoid it. By dedicating time each day to sitting quietly and focusing on my breath, I gradually learned to accept my feelings without being overwhelmed by them. This practice did not eliminate my struggles but provided a way to manage them with greater ease and understanding.

1. What small changes can you make in your daily routine to incorporate mindfulness?
2. How does mindfulness affect your reaction to stress or challenges?
3. Reflect on a time when mindfulness helped you gain clarity. What did you learn from that experience?

Mindful Journeys

- **Breathing Exercise:** Sit comfortably and focus on your breath. Inhale deeply through your nose, hold for a few seconds, and exhale slowly through your mouth. Repeat for five minutes.
- **Mindful Observation:** Take a moment to observe your surroundings. Notice the colors, textures, and sounds without judgment.
- **Gratitude List:** Each day, write down three things you are grateful for. Reflect on how they contribute to your well-being.

Simple Acceptance

Heartbreak leaves us aching,
But mindfulness helps us heal.
In the middle of our flaws,
Self-love starts to feel real.

We don't need to be flawless,
Just honest and kind.
In loving our true selves,
Peace is what we find.

The Art of Self-Acceptance

Self-acceptance is a journey fraught with its own set of challenges. Accepting ourselves fully requires facing our imperfections and understanding that we are not defined by our flaws. This process can be difficult and often feels like an ongoing battle against our inner critic.

The path to self-acceptance involves embracing the parts of ourselves that we might wish to change or hide. It means acknowledging our mistakes and shortcomings without letting them undermine our sense of worth. This can be an uncomfortable and challenging course as it requires us to confront and make peace with aspects of ourselves that we may have long denied.

However, through persistent effort and compassion, self-acceptance becomes a source of profound inner peace. It allows us to move forward with greater confidence and self-love, knowing that our worth is inherent and not contingent on perfection.

Personal Insight:

Learning to accept myself was a deeply transformative experience. I had to confront many aspects of myself that I had previously judged harshly. By practicing self-compassion and focusing on my strengths, I began to embrace my whole self with kindness. This shift not only improved my relationship with myself but also positively impacted my interactions with others.

1. What are some of the negative beliefs you hold about yourself? How can you challenge these beliefs?
2. Write about a time when you accepted yourself despite imperfections. What was the outcome?
3. How does self-acceptance influence your relationships with others?

Mindful Journeys

- **Affirmation Practice:** Create a list of positive affirmations about yourself. Repeat them daily to reinforce your self-worth.
- **Celebrate Achievements:** Keep a journal where you note your accomplishments, no matter how small. Reflect on these achievements regularly.
- **Self-Compassion Breaks:** Take short breaks throughout your day to practice self-compassion. Remind yourself that it's okay to be imperfect.

Understanding

Understanding comes slowly,
Like dawn's gentle light.
It's a journey through shadows,
To embrace what's in sight.

Each step brings new clarity,
A deeper, softer view.
In learning to understand,
We find ourselves anew.

Understanding

The path to understanding ourselves and our experiences is often challenging and gradual. It's a process that requires patience and a willingness to confront the often uncomfortable truths about ourselves. This journey involves digging deep into our emotions and experiences, which can be both enlightening and distressing.

True understanding comes not from quick fixes but from a sustained effort to explore and reflect on our inner world. It involves acknowledging our vulnerabilities, recognizing patterns in our behavior, and accepting our personal truths. It can feel arduous as it often forces us to confront aspects of ourselves that we might prefer to overlook.

Yet, it is through this rigorous process that we gain profound insights into our true selves. This understanding is not a destination but a continuous journey of exploration and self-discovery.

Personal Experience:

I found that understanding myself deeply required a lot of introspection and honest reflection. There were moments when this process was painful and challenging, but it ultimately led to a greater sense of clarity and acceptance. By facing my inner struggles and being open to learning from them, I was able to achieve a more profound self-awareness.

1. How do you currently reflect on your experiences and emotions? What methods might help you gain a deeper understanding?
2. How has seeking feedback from others influenced your self-awareness?
3. Reflect on a moment when understanding yourself or a situation became clearer. What helped you achieve that insight?

Mindful Journeys

- **Self-Reflection Exercise:** Spend 10 minutes reflecting on a recent experience that was challenging. Write about your emotions and what you learned from it.
- **Feedback Journaling:** After receiving feedback, jot down your thoughts and reactions. Reflect on how this feedback might enhance your self-understanding.
- **Insightful Conversations:** Have a conversation with a trusted friend or mentor about a personal challenge. Discuss your perspectives and listen to their insights.

It Takes Time

It takes time to mend a heart,
To find a way to heal.
In the passage of each moment,
Our strength begins to feel.

Patience is a gentle guide,
Through the valleys of our soul.
With each step, we come to know
That time can make us whole.

It Takes Time

The journey through heartache and self-discovery is never instantaneous. It's a process that demands patience and resilience. The experience of emotional pain and the path to healing are both gradual and non-linear.

When facing difficult emotions, it often feels like progress is slow and the road to recovery is long. There are days when it seems as though there is no relief in sight, and the weight of the pain feels unbearable. It is crucial to recognize that these feelings are a normal part of the healing process and that they will eventually pass.

The key is to embrace the passage of time as a healing ally. Each day, no matter how challenging, is a step toward recovery. By practicing patience and maintaining hope, we allow ourselves the grace to heal at our own pace.

Personal Insight:

In my own experience, the passage of time has been both a comfort and a challenge. Healing from a deep emotional wound took longer than I initially anticipated. By focusing on small, manageable steps and practicing patience, I gradually found a sense of peace and resilience. This experience taught me the value of allowing time to work its magic and the importance of being gentle with myself throughout the process.

1. How do you handle the waiting periods in your personal growth and healing process?
2. Reflect on a situation where time played a crucial role in your healing or growth. What did you learn from it?
3. How can you practice patience with yourself during challenging times?

Mindful Journeys

- **Set Small Goals:** Identify a specific area in your life where you want to make progress. Break it down into smaller, achievable goals and track your progress.
- **Patience Journal:** Write about a recent experience where patience was required. Reflect on how it impacted your journey and what you learned.
- **Time Appreciation:** Spend a few moments each day acknowledging and appreciating the time you give yourself for growth and healing.

Realization

In the quiet of our hearts,
Realization blooms,
A light that softly shows us
The wisdom that resumes.

Through trials and reflections,
We come to truly see
The essence of our being
And the path we're meant to be.

The Moment of Realization

Realization often emerges from the depths of struggle and introspection. It's a moment when the fog of confusion clears and we gain a new perspective on our situation or ourselves. These moments are both profound and challenging as they require us to confront truths that may be uncomfortable or surprising.

Experiencing a realization can be transformative, but it often comes after a period of intense reflection and emotional upheaval. The process leading up to such insights can be fraught with difficulty as it involves questioning long-held beliefs and facing uncomfortable truths.

Yet, these realizations offer a path to greater understanding and growth. They can guide us toward new directions, provide clarity, and help us make sense of our experiences. Embracing these moments with openness allows us to integrate them into our journey and move forward with renewed purpose.

Personal Anecdote:

A significant realization in my life came after a period of deep personal reflection. The clarity I gained was initially overwhelming as it challenged many of my previous assumptions and beliefs. However, embracing this new understanding ultimately provided me with a clearer sense of direction and purpose. The journey to this realization was not easy, but it was instrumental in my personal growth and development.

1. What recent realizations have significantly impacted your life or perspective?
2. How do you cultivate an environment that allows for moments of realization and insight?
3. Reflect on a past experience that led to a profound realization. How did it shape your journey?

Mindful Journeys

- **Reflective Practice:** Spend time each week reflecting on your experiences and what they might reveal about your path forward.
- **Insight Journal:** Keep a journal where you record moments of realization and their impact on your life.
- **Open Mind Exercise:** Challenge yourself to explore new experiences or viewpoints. Reflect on how these broaden your understanding of yourself and your journey.

Compassion

Compassion is a gentle touch,
A balm for wounds unseen.
It starts within our own hearts,
A gift that's pure and keen.

To be kind to ourselves first
Is where true healing starts.
In showing love and empathy,
We mend our tender parts.

The Power of Compassion

Compassion is a transformative force that begins with how we treat ourselves. It involves a deep sense of empathy and kindness, both towards others and ourselves. However, many people overlook the importance of extending compassion to themselves, focusing instead on how they interact with others.

The journey of compassion involves recognizing and addressing our own suffering with kindness. It means being gentle with ourselves when we make mistakes or face challenges rather than harshly judging our actions. This internal compassion fosters a more positive and nurturing environment within ourselves.

In practice, compassion helps us develop resilience and a more balanced perspective. By treating ourselves with the same empathy and understanding we offer others, we create a foundation of self-love that supports our emotional well-being and personal growth.

Personal Insight:

Developing compassion for myself was initially challenging as I was accustomed to self-criticism. By consciously practicing self-kindness and forgiving myself for past mistakes, I gradually cultivated a more compassionate inner dialogue. This shift not only improved my self-esteem but also enhanced my ability to empathize with others.

1. How do you practice compassion toward yourself in daily life?
2. Reflect on a time when you were kind to yourself despite feeling undeserving. What was the outcome?
3. How can extending compassion to yourself improve your interactions with others?

Mindful Journeys

- **Self-Compassion Exercise:** Write a letter to yourself offering understanding and kindness about a recent struggle or mistake.
- **Compassion Meditation:** Spend a few minutes each day visualizing yourself surrounded by warmth and kindness. Repeat affirmations of self-love and acceptance.
- **Acts of Kindness:** Perform a small act of kindness for yourself each day, such as taking a relaxing bath or enjoying a favorite hobby.

Kindness

Kindness is a simple act,
A smile or helping hand.
It starts within our own hearts,
A gift that's always planned.

To treat ourselves with kindness
Is the purest form of grace.
In nurturing our own hearts,
We find a peaceful place.

The Essence of Kindness

Kindness is a fundamental yet often overlooked aspect of self-care. It involves treating ourselves with the same consideration and warmth that we extend to others. While kindness towards others is frequently practiced, many people neglect to offer the same courtesy to themselves.

The essence of kindness lies in its simplicity and authenticity. It's about acknowledging our worth and deservingness of care. When we practice kindness toward ourselves, we foster a sense of self-worth and create a more positive internal environment. This, in turn, enhances our ability to be kind to others as our own well-being influences how we interact with the world.

Embracing kindness as a daily practice means making deliberate choices that honor our needs and feelings. It's a conscious effort to nurture ourselves and recognize the importance of self-love as a cornerstone of a fulfilling life.

Personal Experience:

Incorporating kindness into my daily routine was a game-changer. Simple acts, like allowing myself time for rest or treating myself to something special, had a profound impact on my mood and self-esteem. This practice not only improved my self-image but also made me more attuned to the needs of others.

1. How do you show kindness to yourself in your daily life?
2. Reflect on a time when being kind to yourself had a positive impact on your overall well-being.
3. What are some small, achievable acts of kindness you can integrate into your routine?

Mindful Journeys

- **Daily Acts of Kindness:** Identify one small act of kindness you can perform for yourself each day. It could be as simple as taking a moment to relax or enjoying a favorite treat.
- **Kindness Journal:** Keep a journal where you record acts of kindness toward yourself and their effects on your mood and self-esteem.
- **Kindness Challenge:** Challenge yourself to practice kindness toward yourself for a week. Note any changes in your overall outlook and self-perception.

Intimate Healing Awareness

Embrace the Present

When the past feels heavy,
And the future's unclear,
Turn to this moment,
And find solace here.

Feel the breath that grounds you,
The pulse within your veins.
In this simple awareness,
There are no chains.

Shadows and Light

We are woven of shadows,
And threads of bright hue.
Each part tells a story,
Each moment rings true.

Do not fear the darkness,
Nor shy from the pain,
For in every shadow,
The light is sustained.

The Gentle Art of Letting Go

Letting go is not about forgetting or erasing the past but about releasing the grip it has on your present. Imagine carrying a heavy stone; over time, your arms tire, and the weight pulls you down. To let go is to set the stone aside, freeing yourself to move forward.

This process takes courage and trust. Trust that life will offer new joys and lessons and the courage to face the unknown without the burdens of what once was. Begin by acknowledging what you hold on to, and with each breath, allow yourself to release it, piece by piece.

1. What are you holding on to that no longer serves you?
2. How does it feel to imagine setting it down?
3. What small step can you take today toward letting go?

The Mirror Within

Stand before the mirror,
And look into your eyes.
See the strength within you
And all that's yet to rise.

Do not judge too harshly,
The face that stares back,
For it's the sum of journeys,
The courage you don't lack.

Honoring Your Journey

Each step of your life's journey has led you to this moment. While it's tempting to dwell on missteps or regrets, remember that every experience contributes to your growth. Honor your path, both the smooth and the rocky roads, for they've shaped the resilient person you are today.

1. What moments in your journey are you most grateful for?
2. How can you show gratitude for lessons learned from challenges?
3. What aspect of your journey do you need to honor more fully?

The Ocean of Healing

Dive deep into yourself,
Where the waters run clear.
In the ocean of healing,
You'll find what's dear.

Each ripple a whisper,
Each wave a soft guide,
Let the currents lead you
To peace deep inside.

Final Wish

As you step away from these pages, may you carry with you a renewed sense of hope and purpose. May you honor the beauty within yourself and approach each day with mindfulness and compassion. This is not the end but the beginning of a lifelong journey toward healing and awareness. Wishing you peace, growth, and joy on this transformative path.

Author Bio

Adelina is a former Miss Malaysia titleholders, AFO radio announcer, and SSI International Mermaid Instructor Trainer. While her life appeared perfect to the outside world, she faced personal challenges in navigating relationships with her parents, friends, and partners.

Through these experiences, Adelina embarked on a journey of self-discovery, overcoming pain and finding clarity. Her debut book reflects this awakening, offering insights to inspire others to heal, embrace their true selves, and rediscover love and gratitude.

With a deep appreciation for nature, animals, and life's interconnectedness, Adelina hopes her story will empower readers to transform their own lives.

www.ingramcontent.com/pod-product-compliance
Lightning Source LLC
Chambersburg PA
CBHW021138130726
47988CB00003B/1357